SAM
WALTON

Founder of the Walmart Empire

CONTENTS

CHAPTER ONE

A NEW OPPORTUNITY

In 1945, Sam Walton was just a young man with a dream. That year, Walton purchased a Ben Franklin franchise in the small town of Newport, Arkansas. Walton was only 27 years old, but he had high hopes for the store and his career. He also had the determination to succeed. At this point in his life, Walton knew he had a future in retail. However, he had a few lessons to learn, and they would not come easily.

Ben Franklin Store

Walton paid $25,000 for his Ben Franklin franchise. Only $5,000 was money he had saved. The other $20,000 he borrowed from his father-in-law, who was very supportive of the endeavor. Walton also had to pay 5 percent of the store's sales to his landlord for renting the store's building.[1] Walton later found out this

Sam Walton, future multibillionaire and cofounder of Walmart, endured early struggles with competitors before finding success.

A SMALL-TOWN START

Before moving to Newport, Walton had a chance to buy a Federated Department Store, another chain owned by Butler Brothers, in Saint Louis, Missouri. Walton was excited about the idea, but his wife, Helen, changed his mind. Helen did not want to live in a big city. She and Walton had already moved 16 times in just the two years they had been married. Helen was willing to put up with moving as long as her husband did not ask her to live in a large city. Newport only had approximately 7,000 people. It was the perfect place for the couple to start out.

was a much higher rent than most store owners in his area were paying.

But in many ways, Walton's first retail management attempt was extremely successful. Ben Franklin was a franchise operated by Butler Brothers, a regional retailer. Ben Franklin stores were variety stores located across the country that sold a mix of household goods at discounted prices. As a franchise, the store was owned by Walton with the support of Butler Brothers. In other words, Walton was allowed to use the brand name "Ben Franklin" and processes for running the store that were established by Butler Brothers. Butler Brothers gave Walton the information he needed to run the store, including products he could buy from Butler Brothers' suppliers and the prices he should offer customers.

In return, Walton had to give a portion of his profits to Butler Brothers.

Although the Butler Brothers' handbook clearly spelled out how Walton should run his Ben Franklin store to make a profit, it was not long before Walton started doing things his own way. Only 80 percent of his merchandise had to be purchased through Butler Brothers.[2] He soon realized he could negotiate cheaper prices for products directly from the seller, rather than going through Butler Brothers. By doing this, Walton

BIRTH OF SELF-SERVICE STORES

When Walton purchased the Ben Franklin, most stores operated a bit differently than they do today. When you shop today, you find the items you want to purchase yourself and bring them up to the cash register to pay for them. But when Walton was starting out, stores had clerks stationed at cash registers throughout the store. A customer would ask a clerk to find the items that he or she needed to buy. The clerk would locate the items, package them, and ring up the total cost for the customer.

The self-service stores that are now common were just beginning to gain popularity as Walton entered the retail management business. Self-service stores saved money because storekeepers did not need to hire as many clerks to assist customers. Many customers also liked being able to pick out their own items and not having to wait for a clerk's help. Walton's Ben Franklin and the Eagle Store he would soon open in Newport operated under the old model. But Walton would eventually be at the forefront of the change to self-service stores.

could offer a lower price to his customers. This helped Walton quickly gain customers in Newport.

Walton also employed other methods to draw in customers. He got a popcorn machine and sold popcorn in front of the store. After this venture proved successful, Walton took out a loan to purchase an ice cream machine, too. That brought even more customers into the store.

Walton was new to the management business, but he had the drive to succeed. In the first year he owned the Ben Franklin, it made $105,000 in sales, a $33,000 improvement from the previous year.[3] Walton seemed well on his way to retail greatness. However, he had a few hurdles left to jump.

The Competition

Walton kept a close eye on his competition in Newport, a habit he would carry with him for life. Walton's main competitor in Newport was another variety store, John Dunham's Sterling store. It was just across the street from Walton's Ben Franklin. Walton would often walk around Dunham's store to scope out his competitor's prices and displays.

Walton began his experience as a retail store owner with a small variety store in Newport, Arkansas, called Ben Franklin, similar to this one.

Then one day Walton discovered the store directly next to Sterling, a Kroger grocery store, planned to sell its lease to Dunham. Dunham was preparing to expand Sterling into the new space. Walton was concerned. If the Sterling store got bigger it would mean more competition for the Ben Franklin. Walton rushed to discuss the issue with the landlady of Kroger's. Walton convinced her to sell the space to him instead of Dunham. At that point, Walton did not know what he would do with the new space—he only knew he could not let Dunham have it.

The Eagle Store

Walton opened a department store called the Eagle Store in the new space. He had always wanted to run a department store, but the Eagle Store was more about preventing competition than anything else. The 2,500-square-foot (762 sq m) store was not very profitable for Walton, but it was not operating at a loss either.[4] Walton believed he had protected the Ben Franklin's business by opening the Eagle Store. But there was another competitor he had overlooked.

When Walton opened the Eagle Store, he began competing with his landlord of the Ben Franklin store, P. K. Holmes, who also owned a department store in town. Walton did not realize he had only a five-year lease for the space the Ben Franklin store occupied. When it came time to renew the lease, Holmes refused to do so. Holmes had seen how successful Walton was, and he did not want Walton's competition in town. Holmes offered to buy the Ben Franklin franchise instead.

"[The Eagle Store] was really the beginning of where Walmart is today. We did everything. We would wash windows, sweep floors, trim windows. We did all the stockroom work, checked the freight in. Everything it took to run a store."[5]
—Bud Walton, Sam Walton's brother and business partner

Walton was furious. He had a lawyer review the lease, but nothing could be done if Holmes did not want to renew it. There was no building in town Walton could move the Ben Franklin into. He was forced to sell the Ben Franklin and its inventory to Holmes. He then sold the Eagle Store to Dunham.

Forced to Start Over

Walton was devastated. He had been so proud of both his stores in Newport, but now he had nothing. His growing family had become involved in community activities and church in Newport. The last thing Walton wanted to do was move his family, but he had no choice.

Although this was a low point in Walton's life, he was not about to give up. He and his family would next settle in Bentonville, Arkansas. There, Walton would start all over again with a new store—Walton's Five & Dime. Little did he know his new venture would be the start of something bigger than anyone could have imagined.

"It was the low point of my business life. I felt sick to my stomach. I couldn't believe it was happening to me. It really was like a nightmare. I had built the best variety store in the whole region and worked hard in the community—done everything right—and now I was being kicked out of town."[6]
—Sam Walton, on losing the Ben Franklin and the Eagle Store in Newport

CHAPTER
TWO

SOUTHERN UPBRINGING

S am Walton grew up in several small southern towns during the Great Depression. The Great Depression was a prolonged period of economic hardship in the United States during the 1930s. Many people struggled to find work and provide for their families. In the atmosphere of the Great Depression, Sam learned the value of money and hard work at an early age.

Childhood

Samuel Moore Walton was born on March 29, 1918. He was the first child of Tom and Nancy, or "Nan," Walton. The family lived on a farm just a few miles from the town of Kingfisher, Oklahoma. Sam was named after his grandfather on his father's side. Three years after Sam's birth, his brother, James "Bud" Walton, was born. James would become Sam's lifelong friend and, eventually, his business partner.

Although he came from humble beginnings, Sam Walton would one day become one of the wealthiest men in the country.

Sam's family was doing well financially when Sam was born. The United States was in the midst of World War I (1914–1918). The government was encouraging farmers to produce more and more crops to feed soldiers. As a farming family, the Waltons profited from these circumstances. But in late 1918, the war ended. This left many US farmers with a surplus of crops. Tom struggled as a farmer for several more years before quitting farming altogether. He moved his family to Springfield, Missouri, and began working for Walton Mortgage Company, which his brother owned. Sam was approximately five years old when the family moved.

More Moves

As the Great Depression began at the end of the 1920s, Tom's job was to repossess farms from families unable to pay their mortgage loans. Sam occasionally accompanied his father on his travels from farm to farm. The work was gloomy because many were losing family farms that had been passed down for generations.

The family lived in Springfield for only a few months before moving to Marshall, Missouri. There, Tom attempted to start his own business in real estate and insurance. Marshall provided Sam with some new experiences as well. Sam joined the Boy Scouts. He already had a competitive attitude—he made a bet with his Boy Scout friends that he would be the first to earn the rank of Eagle Scout. Sam also swam in the summer and played football, basketball, and baseball the rest of the year.

Unfortunately, Tom's new business venture failed due to the poor economic climate. Tom went back to working for Walton Mortgage Company and moved the family to Shelbina, Missouri. There, Sam won his bet with the Boy Scouts when he earned his Eagle designation at age 13. This made him the youngest Eagle Scout in Missouri.

Providing for the Family

Since Sam's family struggled financially, Sam and his brother often worked to help the family. As a kid, Sam helped his mother with her milk business. Sam milked the cows before school, and his mother bottled the milk while he was at school. Then, after Sam came home from football practice in the afternoon, he delivered the milk to customers for ten cents per gallon. Sam and his mother had approximately ten customers.

Besides the milk business, Sam found other ways to make money for his family. When he was eight years old, he began selling magazine subscriptions. Sam also had a successful newspaper route. And, similar to many country boys, Sam raised rabbits and pigeons to sell. Sam later reflected that helping out the family in this way made a lasting impression on him and Bud, saying, "In the process . . . we learned how much hard work it took to get your hands on a dollar, and that when you did it was worth something."[2]

Successful Sam

Sam learned the importance of teamwork at a young age, too, through his experience with organized sports. In fifth grade, Sam joined the peewee football team and competed against neighboring towns. Sam's early experience served him well when his family moved to Shelbina. He was smaller than a lot of his teammates and opponents, but he had more experience. Sam was made second-string quarterback in ninth grade.

Sam's family soon moved again, this time to Columbia, Missouri, where Sam attended Hickman High School. Nan hoped moving Sam and Bud to Columbia would give them a better chance of attending the University of Missouri, which was located in that city. She wanted both her children to be college educated.

Sam continued to succeed in extracurricular activities at his new school in Columbia. He was the quarterback of the school's undefeated football team, the Kewpies, and lettered in basketball, even though he was quite short. Sam enjoyed his experience with sports.

SAVING A LIFE

Sam's Boy Scout training came into serious use during a near tragedy in Shelbina one summer day in 1932. Sam was only 14 years old when he saved a young boy, Donald Peterson, from drowning. The local newspaper, the *Shelbina Democrat*, reported the event:

> Donald got into water too deep for him and called for help. Loy Jones, who had accompanied the boys, made an effort to get him out, but Donald's struggles pulled Mr. Jones down several times. Young Walton, who was some distance away, got to the pair just as Donald went down a fifth time. He grasped him from behind, as he had been taught to do, pulled him to shore, and applied artificial respiration that Scouts must become proficient in.[3]

Sam later reflected that the newspaper might have exaggerated the story. But he recognized he had a "take action" attitude from a very young age.

Sports such as football provided young Walton with the opportunity to excel in a team environment. Later, he would work to promote this team mentality with his Walmart employees.

He felt it taught him about teamwork and how to be a leader.

Young Sam also excelled in his nonathletic pursuits. He did not recall being naturally smart. Rather, he had to work hard to get good grades. Sam made the honor club and participated in his school's speech club.

Sam was also vice president of his junior class. In his senior year, he was voted president of the student body.

Sam was voted "Most Versatile Boy" in the yearbook, and his high school friends later remembered him fondly. Clay Cooper, a fellow student and football player recalled, "Sam was a hard worker. He was optimistic all the time. He had a great smile on his face and felt like everybody was his friend and the world was something he could conquer."[4]

Dreams for the Future

Sam had big plans for his future and knew hard work was the way to success. Sam's mother had dropped out of college to marry Sam's father. She deeply regretted not finishing school and made it clear to her sons they were expected to attend college. Nan hoped Sam would become a lawyer, but as he entered college Sam was considering a career in politics or insurance sales.

Sam was able to get into the University of Missouri. He began his first year there in 1936. Because he was well known around the city from his high school success, he got some benefits that may not have been offered to him otherwise. For example, Beta Theta Pi fraternity accepted Sam due to his reputation as a stellar athlete. During his sophomore year, the fraternity made Sam rush captain. That meant he had to travel the state of Missouri during the summer to interview men who might be allowed to join the fraternity. This gave him more experience in leadership.

Sam's next goal was to become president of the university student body. In his attempts to become well known on campus, Sam further developed his social skills. He realized if he wanted to get to know people, he would have to be the one to speak to them first. He explained in his autobiography,

> I learned early on that one of the secrets to campus leadership was the simplest thing of all: speak to people coming down the sidewalk before they speak to you. . . . I would always look ahead and speak to the person coming toward me. If I knew them, I would call them by name, but even if I didn't I would still speak to them.[5]

Using this technique, Sam was soon one of the most popular students on campus. He started to get elected to more important positions at the university, including the senior men's honor society and president of the senior class. He also became an officer for Beta Theta Pi and the captain and president of Scabbard and Blade, a Reserve Officers' Training Corps (ROTC) organization. This organization allowed commissioned officers of the US armed forces to attend college with a scholarship that covered tuition in part or in full in return for active military service upon graduation. He continued his interest in religion and the church community, becoming president of Burall Bible Class. The class was made up of students from both the University of Missouri and Stephens College.

Making His Own Way

Throughout college, Sam had to pay for his own living expenses. His parents were unable to help him financially. So, in addition to all his other activities, Sam took on several different jobs. He continued his high school job of delivering newspapers. His boss at the time, Ezra Entrekin, remembered Sam's work ethic, saying, "He was good. He was really good. And dedicated."[6] Sam also waited tables at a restaurant and was paid in meals. He found employment as head lifeguard at a local swimming pool. Sam estimated he was making approximately $4,000 per year while in college.[7]

As Sam got ready to graduate with a degree in business in June 1940, he still was not quite sure what he wanted to do with his life. He thought about continuing on to business school at the Wharton School at the University of Pennsylvania. But it was expensive to attend. Sam also felt a need to leave the academic rigor of college. He wanted to start making a solid salary. Retail was not yet on his mind, but his job search would soon take him in that direction.

At the University of Missouri in Columbia, Walton honed his leadership and social skills, becoming involved in several school groups and activities.

CHAPTER
THREE

J. C. PENNEY AND WORLD WAR II

As Walton entered the work world, he did not know what was in store for him. At the same time, trouble was brewing in Europe as World War II (1939–1945) raged on, and the United States was trying to decide whether to get involved. Walton knew he wanted to make something of himself, but he was not entirely sure what that would be yet.

During his senior year at the University of Missouri, Walton had already started looking for a job. He had meetings with representatives from both J. C. Penney and Sears Roebuck when they visited campus. Both companies offered Walton a job. He decided to go with J. C. Penney.

Just days after graduation, on June 3, 1940, Walton reported to the J. C. Penney store in Des Moines, Iowa. He would assist customers and work as a cashier. Walton was eager to start work. He started as a

Upon college graduation, Walton worked for J. C. Penney in Des Moines, Iowa, where he discovered his knack for sales.

management trainee, making $75 a month plus commissions.[1] After training, he became an associate, which was essentially a salesperson in the store.

At J. C. Penney, Walton quickly discovered his talent for selling products to customers. This was a skill he had been perfecting since his childhood days of selling magazines. However, his constant focus on customer service often left other parts of his job unfilled. He had trouble keeping track of his transaction paperwork after he sold something to a customer because he did not want to keep the next customer waiting while he recorded a purchase. Walton also had terrible handwriting, which frustrated some of his supervisors. But since Walton was such a successful salesman, his supervisors mainly overlooked these shortcomings.

Trying hard to stand out at his new job, Walton worked from 6:30 a.m. to 7 p.m. and gave himself only 15 minutes for a lunch break. Walton found a mentor in Duncan Majors, the store's manager. Majors's pride toward the store and its employees motivated Walton. Majors would routinely invite Walton and other

J. C. Penney associates to his home on Sundays to visit and talk about business. Since Walton enjoyed retail so much, he began setting his sights on reaching a management position.

War Shifts Plans

Just as Walton was moving forward with his retail career, the United States entered World War II after the Japanese attack on Pearl Harbor in Hawaii on December 7, 1941. Having participated in ROTC, Walton expected he would fight in the war. So, in early 1942, he reported for the mandatory physical exam needed for combat. Much to Walton's dismay, the doctor discovered Walton had a minor heart issue. It would not likely affect Walton's general health, but it made him unsuitable for combat. However, the army

HIDDEN ROMANCE

While working at J. C. Penney, Walton dated Beth Hamquist, a young woman who worked as a cashier at the store. But in those days, J. C. Penney had a policy against employees dating other employees. The company was concerned that relationships between employees could cause morale problems. Hamquist and Walton had to hide their relationship from other workers.

After dating for a while, Hamquist believed Walton planned to propose to her, but he did not. Eventually, Walton had to break the news to Beth that he did not want to marry her. Walton would later include rules against employees dating each other when he opened his own stores.

HELEN ROBSON

Walton's wife, Helen, came from a hardworking and wealthy family. Helen's father was a lawyer, rancher, and banker. He impressed upon Helen and her three brothers the importance of being careful with money.

Helen was a successful young woman. She had been the valedictorian of her high school and went to Christian College in Columbia, Missouri, for two years before transferring and completing her degree in economics at the University of Oklahoma at Norman. After college, she worked at her father's law office and managed the finances for her family's ranch. Her background made her a perfect match for the equally ambitious Walton.

could still use Walton in a noncombat position.

Still, Walton was depressed and waited to be called to serve in the war. After 18 months at J. C. Penney, he quit his job, believing he would soon be called for noncombatant training. He traveled to Tulsa, Oklahoma, because he was interested in the oil business there. He ended up with a job at a gunpowder plant in Pryor, a town near Tulsa.

While working in Pryor, Walton rented a place to live in Claremore, another neighboring town. It was there Walton met his future wife, Helen Robson. They met one April night when Walton was at a bowling alley with some friends. Helen was there on a date with another young man. Walton recognized Helen because he had dated a friend of Helen's from college. Walton asked Helen for the other girl's number

Walton met Helen Robson, his future wife, in Claremore, Oklahoma. In later years, Helen encouraged Walton to establish a philanthropic foundation.

so he could get back in touch, but pretty soon he was dating Helen instead. The two young people fell in love. Walton admired Helen's ambition and intelligence. Unfortunately for the new couple, Walton was soon called to army training.

Due to his ROTC training, Walton became a second lieutenant, an entry-level commissioned officer typically

The Waltons, pictured with their four children: Alice, John, Jim, and Rob

placed in command of a platoon of soldiers. Walton oversaw prisoner-of-war camps and aircraft stations in California and Utah during the war. With any free time he had, he would read books about retail. While he was in Salt Lake City, Utah, he scoped out the Mormon Church's department store for ideas he might use in the future.

Starting a Family

On Valentine's Day in 1943, Walton took a three-day leave to marry Helen in Oklahoma. On October 28, 1944, Helen gave birth to a baby boy, whom the couple named Samuel Robson Walton. They called him Rob.

Luckily, Walton did not have to be away from his growing family for much longer. Two days after the end of World War II in August 1945, Walton was discharged from his duties. The young Walton family planned to move to a new town, and Walton was eager to find a new opportunity in the retail market. This would lead the family to Newport, Arkansas. There, the Walton family would expand with children John Thomas (1946), James Carr (1948), and Alice Louise (1949). And Walton would first try his hand at retail management with the Ben Franklin store.

J. C. PENNEY IN THE 1940s

When Walton arrived at J. C. Penney in Des Moines in 1940, the company had 1,586 stores across the United States. Overall, the company was making approximately $300 million annually.[3] At this time, J. C. Penney's stores had the most success selling fabric products such as sheets, hosiery, and clothing.

Rather than clerks or employees, J. C. Penney only had associates. The term *associates* made workers feel as if they were more important to the company. Walton would later use this term for workers in Walmarts across the country.

At J. C. Penney, beginning associates, including Walton, were provided with a copy of the "Penney Idea," which was a set of seven guidelines for being a good worker, first conceived in 1913. The "Penney Idea" focused strongly on the importance of excellent customer service and improving oneself as a salesperson. But it also emphasized the importance of being fair to the customer. The seventh guideline in the "Penney Idea" states associates should strive, "To test our every policy, method, and act in this wise: 'Does it square with what is right and just?'"[4]

CHAPTER
FOUR

A SECOND TRY

In 1950, Walton and his family were forced out of Newport, Arkansas, when the landlord of the Ben Franklin franchise Walton owned refused to renew the building's five-year lease. There were no open store spaces in Newport. Walton decided it would be best to strike out with a new store in another town.

A New Store

After a lot of searching, Walton and his family decided on the small town of Bentonville, Arkansas. There were already three variety stores in Bentonville, but Walton was motivated by the competition. He purchased an old Harrison's Variety Store, but it was not quite large enough for his store. Walton obtained a 99-year lease on the barbershop next to Harrison's Variety Store and knocked out the wall between to expand the store space. The new store was named Walton's Five and Dime, although it was technically a Ben Franklin franchise.

Walton's Five and Dime variety store in Bentonville, Arkansas, now serves as the Walmart Visitor Center and displays exhibits tracing the growth of Walmart.

WALTON'S CHILDREN

While Walton began his career as a retail manager in Newport, Arkansas, he and Helen continued to add to their family. On October 8, 1946, the couple's second son, John Thomas Walton, was born. Then James Carr Walton was born on June 7, 1948. Alice Walton, the couple's only daughter, was born on October 7, 1949.

Because Walton worked long hours, much of the child-caring responsibilities fell to Helen. But Walton always looked out for his children and their financial futures. When he became successful with Walmart, he gave all his children shares in the company. Of course, he also required them to contribute to the family business through hard work.

Walton and his family set to work getting the store ready for consumers. Walton relied on the help of Charlie Baum, a friend who had helped him fix up the Eagle Store back in Newport. But Walton's Five and Dime would be a bit different from other stores Walton had managed. Walton had heard of a new type of store model called self-service. He had taken a trip to see two stores in Minnesota using this revolutionary new model. Self-service stores are like stores today where the registers are at the front of the store and customers pick out their own merchandise. Walton liked this idea and decided to use it in his new store. Walton's Five and Dime would be only the third variety store in the United States to use the self-service model. It was a first for Arkansas.

More Stores

Learning from his experiences in Newport, Walton wanted to open stores in other cities. By 1952, he had opened another Walton's Five and Dime in Fayetteville, Arkansas. Unlike the Bentonville store, this store was not a Ben Franklin franchise. Walton needed someone to manage the Fayetteville store. He hired his first manager, Willard Walker.

Walton did not stop after Fayetteville. He soon opened a Ben Franklin in Versailles, Missouri, with his brother, Bud. But even with other managers, Walton liked to be kept informed on the day-to-day operations of all three stores. He liked to stop by and check on them. Walton needed a way to travel quickly between the stores, so he purchased and

A CHANGE FOR THE WALTONS

Moving from Newport to Bentonville was a big change for the Waltons. They had become very involved in the community in Newport, and Bentonville was an even smaller town. Helen remembered her misgivings about the move, but also her hope for a new start, saying, "Bentonville really was just a sad-looking country town, even though it had a railroad track to it. . . . I couldn't believe this was where we were going to live. It only had 3,000 people, compared to Newport, which was a thriving cotton and railroad town of 7,000 people. . . . But I knew after we got here that it was going to work out."[1]

As he opened more stores and expanded his business travel, Walton purchased this small airplane and learned to fly it to get between his stores quickly.

learned to fly an airplane. Then Walton expanded his reach even farther, opening more variety stores in cities including Little Rock, Springdale, and Siloam Spring in Arkansas and in Neodesha and Coffeyville in Kansas.

Even though the stores were successful, Walton was already thinking of his next step. Always researching and studying different types of store models, Walton heard about a new trend of giant discount stores. He was intrigued, but he was also worried. Walton saw potential for these big stores, but he also saw them as a threat to his current stores. If the giant discounts became very popular, they would run the type of variety store Walton owned to the ground. In order to stay profitable, he had to adapt to the changing market.

TORNADO HITS

Walton was proud of the Ben Franklin store he and Bud shared in Versailles, Missouri. It was part of a shopping center, which was a brand-new concept at the time. The shopping center turned out to be very successful. But on May 20, 1957, a tornado hit the town of Versailles. Bud called and told Walton he did not think the damage from the storm had been too bad, although he had not yet seen the store. But Walton was worried. Since he was unable to contact anyone at the store to check on the damage, he hurriedly drove out to Versailles to check for himself.

When Walton arrived at the store at two o'clock in the morning, he was shocked to see it was nearly leveled. Fortunately, none of the employees were seriously hurt and the store was insured. But it was still an emotional blow to both brothers, especially because it happened so quickly. Walton remembered, "It was there one minute and gone the next."[2] They rebuilt the store and continued business as usual, but Walton never forgot how quickly the store was lost.

A New Venture: The First Walmart

Walton wanted to move toward owning a giant discount store, but he appreciated the security he got from franchises. He liked the support of companies such as Butler Brothers. So, he pitched his idea for his own giant discounting store to Butler Brothers. He wanted them to be the merchandiser for his new store. Despite Walton's known success with the franchise, Butler Brothers did not want to get involved. Walton would not be able to rely on a franchise company. He would have to create his own company to back his new discount store.

Walton had decided to build his new store in Rogers, Arkansas. But in order to build and open the store, he had to put down 95 percent of the money for it.[4] The rest came from friends and family who invested in the venture. It was a big risk for Walton because he had to take out a large amount in loans. But he was confident this type of store was the wave of the future.

On July 2, 1962, Walton opened the first Walmart in Rogers. Because the main goal of the store was to provide goods at highly discounted prices, not much money was spent on making the store look appealing or fancy. The store's floor was made with plain concrete. It was more like a barn or a warehouse than the Walmarts around today. Merchandise was categorized by type and piled high throughout the store. Walton hoped price alone, not appearance, would bring in customers.

Walton was right. The first Walmart did fairly well, making $700,000 in sales during its first year.[5] But it was not a smashing success. After two years of steady

THE EVOLUTION OF WALMART'S NAME

Sam Walton named his first large discount store Wal-Mart. However, the Walmart name and logo have evolved over time, and his storefronts have displayed signs that read Wal-Mart, Walmart, and even Wal*Mart. A variety of different lettering styles and logo designs has come and gone over the years, however, the stores' promises of "Satisfaction Guaranteed" and "We Sell for Less" have remained constant. Currently, the name of the corporation itself is Wal-Mart Stores, Inc., while the stores carry the spelling Walmart.

The first Walmart opened in Rogers, Arkansas, in 1962. Today, there are more than 10,000 Walmart retail locations throughout the world.

sales, Walton branched out and opened two new Arkansas Walmart stores—one in the larger town of Springdale and the other in the small town of Harrison. Although others remained skeptical, Walton was confident Walmart would bring great success.

KEEPING IT CHEAP

The first Walmart claimed in its newspaper advertisements that it sold only high-quality merchandise. But this was not entirely true. Walton did not care that much about the quality of the products he sold. Because the store hoped to draw in customers with discounted prices, sometimes quality was sacrificed for a good price. Also, since Walton's store was just starting out, it did not yet have a reputation that would allow Walton to buy products from large manufacturers to sell in the store.

Walton also kept prices low for customers through lower salaries for employees. The first Walmart had a total of 25 workers. Most of them were women. They were paid approximately 50¢ per hour. The federal minimum wage at the time was $1.15 per hour.[6] Walton later admitted he probably paid his first employees less than he should have.

CHAPTER
FIVE

WALMART EXPANDS

Although the first Walmart was not an overwhelming success, Walton moved forward with his gut feeling that Walmart could be very successful, and he opened two new Walmart stores in Arkansas. All three Walmarts were located in relatively small towns. It had previously been thought there was not much business in small towns simply because fewer people lived or visited there. But Walton was finding the opposite to be true. He later reflected, "There was much, much more business out there in small-town America than anybody, including me, had ever dreamed of."[1]

No End in Sight

As the market for Walmart stores increased, Walton opened even more stores. While other big retailers were more likely opening a store in a big city or suburb,

Throughout his career, Walton increased his business by following his intuition and hiring diligent, customer-minded employees.

Walton continued opening stores in small, rural towns. Walton opened the fourth Walmart in 1965 and did not stop there. Between 1966 and 1967, Walton opened four more Walmarts. Then, he opened ten more Walmarts in the next two years. By the end of the 1960s, Walton had 18 Walmarts in addition to 14 other variety stores, nine of which were Ben Franklin franchises.[2] Walmart's popularity was clearly growing. Most of these first Walmarts were in Arkansas, but two were in Oklahoma and five in Missouri. As the founder of the Walmart enterprise, Walton became the chairman and chief executive officer (CEO) of Walmart. This made him the last word on decisions made about the company.

In the late 1960s, Walton had a merchandise warehouse and company headquarters built in Bentonville. The original company headquarters, already

"It was the worst retail store I had ever seen. Sam had brought a couple of trucks of watermelons in and stacked them on the sidewalk. He had a donkey ride out in the parking lot. It was about 115 degrees, and the watermelons began to pop, and the donkey began to do what donkeys do, and it all mixed together and ran all over the parking lot. And when you went inside the store, the mess just continued, having been tracked in all over the floor. He was a nice fellow, but I wrote him off. It was just terrible."[3]
—David Glass, who would one day be Walton's business partner, on his first impression of the Harrison Walmart

located in Bentonville, were getting overcrowded as the company quickly grew. The original plans for the new building indicated it would be 100,000 square feet (30,480 sq m). But Walton quickly cut it down to 60,000 square feet (5,574 sq m).[4] He did not believe so much space was needed, and anywhere he could find to cut costs, he always did.

Going His Own Way

As Walmart grew, Walton refused to base his business decisions on the way things were usually done in retail. Instead, he relied on his gut and knowledge of the retail industry to make decisions about running Walmart. He was always willing to learn how other stores operated. If he thought they had a good idea, he used it himself. But if he thought he could do something better, he tried his way instead. Walton also stressed the importance of customer service. He wanted his employees to be knowledgeable about the products they sold and helpful in explaining them to customers. To beat the competition, Walton knew customer service was key.

Walton hired more managers for the stores and people to help with finances and merchandise ordering. Luckily, Walton had a knack for finding hard workers. Unlike most retailers at the time, Walton did not necessarily care whether a potential employee had a lot of education. He just looked for people he thought would work diligently. He sometimes even visited other stores to scope out people to hire. He explained, "[We] looked for action-oriented, do-it-now, go type of folks."[6] Walton also tended to hire people with a competitive spirit. He encouraged managers to create their own promotions to sell more products.

As the company grew, Walton and his business partners started traveling to New York City to purchase merchandise for the Walmart stores. But Walmart was still a small company without much national recognition, so some sellers would not sell products to it. Walton and his buyers also bought merchandise differently from other chains. Buyers will usually purchase one line of merchandise. For example, they might purchase all the kitchenware available from a certain brand. But Walton and his buyers usually bought by item rather than by product line.

On these New York City trips, Walton insisted they do things their own way. He felt the expenses of the trip should not amount to more than 1 percent of the money they planned to spend on purchases. Walmart buyers along for the trip would be crowded into motel rooms, and they would walk to appointments rather than taking taxis.

Walton would also try to keep the group working for the entire trip with few breaks. He would try to find manufacturers that would meet with the group outside of normal business hours. Sometimes this got the group up early and kept them up late into the night. Gary

Reinboth, an early store manager, remembered some early-morning appointments with manufacturers:

> Walton would talk some janitor or somebody into letting us in the building, and we'd be sitting there outside the showroom when those folks started coming in to work. . . . I think he was trying to make a point: just because we're in New York doesn't mean we have to start doing things their way.[8]

TRIAL AND ERROR

Although Walton had several years of franchise experience under his belt, he still had a lot to learn. Walton was also used to doing business in the South. As Walmart expanded across the country, Walton was forced to learn about different retail markets. Sometimes he had to learn the hard way, such as in the case of Moon Pies.

In the South, Walmart had been very successful in selling Moon Pies. Moon Pies were a popular marshmallow snack in the South. Offering customers lower prices, Walmart sold 500,000 Moon Pies in just one week.[9] It was one of the company's best-selling items. Encouraged by the success, Walton shipped Moon Pies to a Walmart in Wisconsin. But the snack was not yet popular in the Midwest. People in Wisconsin did not even know what a Moon Pie was. In comparison to the South, the Moon Pies sales in Wisconsin fell flat. This reminded Walton of the changing nature of his company and how important it was to stay informed on regional trends.

Expecting the Best

Walton required a lot from the people who worked for him. But Walton did not expect more from his employees than he did from himself. He had always been a hard worker, and as Walmart grew, he only worked harder. He quit some of the community activities he had been involved in for years, including his work on the city council in Bentonville. Waking up most days by 4 a.m., Walton threw himself into his day-to-day work schedule. He spent his days visiting his stores, the Walmarts and the Ben Franklins as well as the variety stores he still owned.

While employees mainly respected Walton, they were sometimes bothered by his demanding attitude and their rigorous work schedule. One early manager remembered, "If you did your job for him, he'd pay you well. . . . He was very tough on people."[10]

Walton also expected his children to help out in his stores. Walton's son Rob remembered, "We always worked in the stores. I would sweep the floors and carry boxes after school, even more in the summer."[11] Walton's children were given a small allowance for the work they completed for the family business. Walton

Jim, Alice, and Rob Walton, pictured above, as well as John, who died in 2005, worked for their father when they were young and later become involved in Walmart's corporate and philanthropic endeavors.

wanted to bring them up understanding the value of diligent work. But, unlike how he sometimes treated his regular employees, Walton prided himself in never pushing his children too hard. He wanted them to go after their dreams, even if it differed from the family retail business. As long as they put forth their best effort, Walton was proud of them. By the late 1960s, Walton's children were headed off to college and their own careers, although they would all keep some involvement in the Walmart enterprise.

Staying Competitive

In order to remain viable in a new, changing market, Walton was always looking out for the next new thing in retail. In the 1960s, early types of computers were slowly starting to be used in the retail business for record keeping and data tracking. Walton did not know much about computers, so in 1966 he enrolled in an IBM school specially aimed at retailers and located in Poughkeepsie, New York. But Walton had an alternate reason for going to school. He wanted to find people who were more knowledgeable about technology than he was.

While at the IBM school, Walton saw Abe Marks, who was part of the National Mass Retailers' Institute (NMRI), give a speech and quickly made a connection with him afterward. Marks was impressed with Walton's success despite never having heard of him or Walmart before. He invited Walton to join the NMRI, which turned out to be a great resource for Walton.

Walton also met Ron Mayer, who would become vice president for finance and distribution in 1968.

HESITANT ABOUT TECHNOLOGY

Although Walton recognized that embracing new technology would be important in moving his company forward, he still had some reservations. Mostly, Walton was concerned about costs. Walton also felt if he acted skeptical about technology his employees would work harder to show him how well it could work. He felt this would lead them to create even better ways to do things at Walmart.

Mayer would be at the forefront of moving Walmart into the budding technology age. However, Walton had worries. Having carefully built his company from the ground up, he was now in massive debt. This deeply concerned him. He had always been a frugal person. Walton had to find a way to get his finances sorted out—and soon.

Walton proved to be a savvy businessman, keeping his
operating costs as low as possible and expecting his
associates to make the most efficient use of their time.

8% NET PRE
R EVER"

CHAPTER
SIX

GROWTH STRATEGY

Although Walton had built a successful chain of Walmart stores, he had to take out millions of dollars in loans to do so. Being in debt worried the penny-pinching Walton. He did not want to take on any more debt, but he wanted to continue to expand the company. So, in the late 1960s, Walton started to consider taking the company public. Privately owned companies do this by selling shares of stock to people in the general public who are interested in investing money in the company. If the company does well, investors can make money through their shares. As an added bonus, more investors holding smaller portions of the company would make it more secure.

After discussing the matter with Bud, Walton realized his stores were not profitable enough to allow him to both pay off his debts and continue expanding and building more stores. But Walton was not ready to stop expanding. So he and Bud decided the time was right to take Walmart public. After a lot of

In 1984, Walton danced the hula on Wall Street after his store managers won a challenge to increase sales.

promotion and a pause to wait for the market to be in a good condition, Walmart became a public company on October 1, 1970. Walton's family still owned 61 percent, and therefore still controlled the decisions about the company because they held the majority of the shareholders' votes.[1] It was a huge weight off Walton's shoulders not to be personally financing the company anymore. It also meant he could finally get out of debt.

More Small Towns, More Big Growth

Now that the company was public, Walton could focus on opening more new stores and turning even larger profits. To expand, the company stuck to the same model that was already working well. They brought Walmarts to small towns, offered outstandingly low prices, and relied strongly on word-of-mouth to bring in customers. As always, employees were taught to provide unparalleled customer service. Walton had a saying he called "Wal-Mart's Golden Rule." The rule states, "Number one, the customer is always right; number two, if the customer isn't right, refer to rule number one."[3]

But Walmart remained firmly rooted in the South for some time. Walton liked that he and other managers could easily check up on the stores, which was only possible when they weren't too far away from the Walmart headquarters in Bentonville. Also, any new stores needed to be a day's drive or less away from one of Walmart's warehouses, which he continued to build as more stores opened up.

As Walmart stores became more and more successful, Walton slowly began selling off his Ben Franklin and other non-Walmart stores. He had 16 of these stores in 1968, but by 1972 there were only nine. Walton sold more in the next two years. In 1974, only two of these stores remained.[4] By 1976, all Walton's Ben Franklins had been sold or closed down. It may have been bittersweet, but Walton was always focused on staying on top of retail trends. Variety stores had quickly become a thing of the past.

Changes and Trials in Leadership

By 1974, Walmart had 78 stores across six states, and the company planned to add 24 more Walmarts by the year's end.[5] As more people got involved in the company, Walton became less involved. Walton was still the chairman and CEO of the company, but he had a lot more help than he had in the early days. Now 56 years old, Walton began to take some time off. He and Helen started taking trips together. But Walton felt uneasy about being away from the day-to-day activities of the company. And on trips, he was always sneaking away to check out the local stores.

As Walton started thinking about naming someone to take over for him when he retired, he had several options. Mayer, who Walton had originally hired to help take the company into the digital age, had gained more authority within the company in recent years and was now sharing the executive vice president position with Ferold Arend, who had been with the company longer. Mayer handled Walmart's finance and distribution while Arend worked with its merchandising.

Walton respected both Mayer and Arend. Mayer had made it clear he wanted to eventually become the CEO and chairman of Walmart. Walton felt it was time for him to slow down a little. Also, he knew Mayer would eventually leave the company if he was not made CEO. So in November 1974, Walton decided to resign and give his positions to Mayer. Walton then became the chairman of the executive committee. He would still have authority, but to a much less degree.

But Walton almost immediately had trouble with this transition at work. He kept doing many of the same tasks he had done as CEO even though it was really Mayer's job. At the same time, leadership in the company started dividing into two groups. Many of

KEEPING HIS HOBBIES

Despite the overwhelming success of Walmart and the money that came with it, Walton did not feel tempted to drastically change his way of life. He still enjoyed the same hobbies he had all his life, particularly quail hunting. Walton had several hunting dogs he enjoyed training himself, although other people with his fortune might have paid professional trainers to take care of this for them.

Bud recalled being invited to a fancy quail hunt in Georgia with Walton. Walton, of course, was not a fan of this way of hunting and did things his own way. Bud remembered:

> They told us they'd pick us up at this landing strip. So we flew in there, and there were all these corporate jets lined up. Well, this guy in a Mercedes pulls up to get us. You should've seen the look on his face when Sam opened up the back of that plane, and his five dogs came flyin' out of there. They weren't expecting anybody to bring their own dogs. They had to haul them in that Mercedes.[6]

WALMART CHEER

Walton claimed to deeply dislike disharmony with his company. He wanted his workers to have fun on the job and be friendly to customers. Walton remembered the camaraderie he felt when playing on sports teams as a kid, and he wanted Walmart associates to feel that way about working at his stores. So, Walton had a cheer he sometimes used to rally employees when he visited a Walmart. The cheer spells out the word *Walmart*. It ends with one of Walmart's most important values, *"Who's number one? THE CUSTOMER!"*[8]

the technology experts and others Mayer hired were loyal to him. On the other side, many original store managers teamed up with Arend. Walton felt divided between the two groups, and the split caused a lot of tension for everyone. Arend remembered:

[Walton] always felt the need for his people to compete with one another because he thought it brought out the best in them, and most of the time it did. But this was a situation that just didn't work. When he stepped aside, it created a tough situation for everybody. Ron's people were loyal to him, and mine were loyal to me. Sam was saying, "I'll decide the things that need tiebreakers." That turned out to be a lot more things than he had intended.[7]

Walton took a lot of responsibility for the division in the company. Once he realized how bad it was, he got right to work trying to fix it. On a Saturday evening in June 1976, Walton told Mayer he wanted his old job back and wanted to give Mayer the job of vice chairman and chief financial officer. Mayer had no choice but to give the job back, but he refused Walton's new offer. Walton recalled, "My proposal wasn't agreeable to [Mayer], and I can certainly understand why. He wanted to run the company, and when he couldn't he decided to leave us."[9]

Backlash

Unfortunately, when Mayer left the company, a lot of the people who had been loyal to him left too. The public began doubting whether Walmart could stay successful in the wake of such drastic change. Its stock dropped. But Walton knew Walmart was made great by its principles, not by

APPRECIATION FOR WORKERS

Although Walton in some ways forced Mayer to leave the company, it is clear he had a great appreciation for those who worked for him and helped bring the company to new heights. In his autobiography, Walton described some of the company's top executives: "We had [Don] Whitakers, straight out of the get-after-it-and-stay-after-it old school, to help us get started; Ferold Arend, a methodical, hardworking German, to get us organized; Ron Mayer, a whiz at computers, to get our systems going; Jack Shewmaker, a brilliant shoot-from-the-hip executive with a store manager's mentality, to blow us out of ruts and push us into new ideas we needed to be working with; and David Glass, who could step up in a crisis, keep his cool, and eventually get control of a company that became so big it was hard to comprehend."[10]

the people in charge. Walton promoted Jack Shewmaker to vice president of operations, personnel, and merchandise, confident in him because of the contributions he had already made to the company. Walton hoped Shewmaker would calm things among the group. But not everyone was pleased with the choice, and several more people left the company.

At the same time, Walton contacted David Glass, who had been following Walmart's success since the beginning. Walton had wanted Glass to work for Walmart during its early days. But Glass had turned him down. Now, Walton offered Glass the job of executive vice president of finance and distribution, and he accepted. Walton thought highly of both Glass and Shewmaker. But in some ways he pitted Glass and Shewmaker against each other, encouraging them to compete. With Walton entering his sixties, both Glass

In order to rally superb customer service, Walton believed in keeping a fun work environment for his employees, complete with employee cheers.

and Shewmaker vied to be Walton's successor. Walton insisted he never meant to incite a rivalry.

Despite the rivalry, Glass and Shewmaker eventually eased the tension in the company. But Walton would soon face a greater, personal challenge.

CHAPTER
SEVEN

NEW ENTERPRISES, NEW CHALLENGES

With the Walmart executives working together smoothly again, Walton turned his attention to new projects. Walton was always interested in what the retail market was doing, and he never stopped learning. However, he was soon faced with a completely different type of challenge.

Frightening News

In 1982, Walton had begun feeling more tired and dragged down than usual. He was used to working long hours, but he suddenly struggled to keep up with them. He cut back on his responsibilities at work, but it did not seem to help.

Walton reluctantly went to see a doctor. He was shocked by the diagnosis. Walton had hairy cell leukemia, a rare type of cancer. This cancer destroys white blood cells, and Walton's doctors confirmed his

At the age of 64, Walton was forced to take on a new battle—the fight to conquer cancer.

white blood cell count was very low. The disease was life threatening. In October, Walton wrote a letter in the company newsletter *Walmart World* notifying everyone of his diagnosis. Despite being unsure of his treatment plan at the time, he remained optimistic in his letter, writing, "I'm completely confident . . . that with the right treatment I'll be able to continue doing the things I enjoy most for at least another 20 or 25 years."[1]

TAKING A RISK WITH INTERFERON

When Walton decided to be treated with interferon for his hairy cell leukemia, he was taking a risk. The treatment was very new. When Walton was considering the treatment, only approximately ten patients had tried the drug. Walton made at least three different trips to discuss the use of interferon with the doctors administering it. When he finally made his decision, he was taking a leap of faith.

Walton did not like doctors, so deciding how to treat his illness was difficult for him. He received a consultation from doctors at M. D. Anderson Hospital in Houston, Texas. It was then known as the best cancer treatment center in the country. After some indecision, Walton decided to enter a new trial treatment program using a drug called interferon. The drug had to be injected by needles. There was no firm guarantee it would help his condition, and since it was a new treatment Walton risked dangerous side effects.

But Walton was lucky. He did not experience any side effects. Better still, after a few months of treatment, the cancer went into remission, meaning it was no longer actively growing in his body. Some of his doctors attributed interferon to this success. Others said it was unclear whether the same results could have happened if Walton had not been treated at all. But whatever the reason, by December 1984, Walton was feeling much better.

Sam's Wholesale Club

When his cancer was in remission and he was feeling better, Walton kept working as he always had. His next project would be opening a massive wholesale store. But first, he needed to do his research.

Just as with Walmart, Walton and his business partners created Sam's Wholesale Club out of a concept that already existed. Sol Price had started Price Club stores in 1976 in San Diego, California. The store was first designed to sell bulk products to small businesses but eventually allowed people to become members of the "club" and purchase bulk goods at a discount.

These stores were a good deal for the buyer because merchandise was marked up only approximately 10 percent from the manufacturer's price. Usually goods are marked up 12 to 15 percent.

In 1983, Walton and his son Rob went to visit Price in San Diego. Walton did not tell Price he was planning to copy his store idea. Walton was encouraged by what he learned from Price. A wholesale club seemed like a great idea.

When Walton returned from the trip, the company purchased a large warehouse in Oklahoma City, Oklahoma. They converted it into the first Sam's Wholesale Club. It looked somewhat like a Walmart but much larger. Shipping pallets of goods were stacked up to the 15-foot (4.6 m) ceilings. The first Sam's Club opened to customers in 1983. The store offered goods at prices that were only 9 to 12 percent higher than the manufacturer's price.[2] Members paid an annual fee and had to show special identification cards to be allowed to shop at the store. For some people, such as Walmart stockholders and certain organizations,

> "[Walton] phoned to tell me he was going to start a wholesale club. It was no surprise. He is notorious for looking at what everybody else does, taking the best of it, and then making it better."[3]
>
> —Sol Price, founder of Price Club

Offering members larger discounts on products, Sam's Club stores have continued rising in popularity and now number more than 600 in the United States.

including school systems and hospitals, the membership fee was waived and the customer paid a small extra charge on the regular price of all items.

Walton enjoyed trying something new and felt some of the same anxiety and excitement he had felt when Walmart had just gotten off the ground. But Sam's Club quickly proved successful. As 1983 came to a close, there were three Sam's Clubs up and running. Together, they made $37 million in sales that year. The company's goal had been $25 million. By 1990, 105 Sam's Clubs were in operation across the country. They were making more than $5 billion per year.[4] Walton's new enterprise had surpassed his wildest dreams.

The Glass and Shewmaker Switch

Even as Walton's company became more successful, another corporate shake-up was on the horizon. Walton called both Glass and Shewmaker into his office one summer day in 1984. Neither executive could have prepared for what happened next. Walton told the men he was switching their jobs. This was a positive move for Glass, since he would now be the new president and chief operating officer. But for Shewmaker, his

GLASS AND WALTON

It was clear Walton deeply respected Glass and his position and future with the company. In February 1985, Glass suffered a heart attack at his home. His wife took him to the hospital. When Walton heard about Glass's heart attack, he rushed to the hospital. Upon hearing about the seriousness of the heart attack, Walton had Glass flown to a more reputable heart hospital in Tulsa, Oklahoma. While Glass was there, Walton stayed in a motel in Tulsa.

The Tulsa cardiologists thought Glass should have bypass surgery. But Glass had never had a surgery before and wanted to avoid it if possible. Walton, worried about his friend, went to work getting Glass the best cardiologists in the country for a second opinion. Glass was seen at the University of Texas Medical Center in Houston. There, the doctors decided surgery was not necessary. Walton knew how important Glass was to the company and cared for him like a friend.

David Glass served as Walmart's CEO from 1984 to 2000. He currently owns the Kansas City Royals Major League Baseball team.

status stayed at the same level as before, just in a different position.

Walton refused to discuss the reason for the switch, but many speculated Walton was trying to decide on his successor. The switch led many to believe that Glass would be Walmart's next CEO.

Superstores

In the early 1980s, Walton traveled around the world looking at different types of stores to try to determine what the next big thing in the United States would be. He noticed the success of Carrefours stores in Brazil. These were huge stores that sold both groceries and merchandise. Walton thought these superstores were the wave of the future.

When Walton returned home he started pushing the idea of opening stores in the United States that used the Carrefours concept. In December 1987, on the day after Christmas, Walton opened a Hypermart USA store near Dallas, Texas. This giant store sold both groceries and general merchandise. That same year the company opened three more

Hypermarts, including another in Texas, one in Topeka, Kansas, and the third in Kansas City, Missouri. The stores were not extremely successful, but they laid the groundwork for the Walmart Supercenters that would come later.

Around this same time Walmart experimented with other types of stores as well. They had a small chain of discount drug stores that did not prove very successful. However, the regular Walmart stores were still going strong.

HYPERMART USA

The first Hypermart USA, which opened in the Dallas-Fort Worth area of Texas in 1987, caused quite a stir. The store was giant. It offered three times the merchandise available at Walmart as well as grocery items. A story in the *New York Times* reported the store was large enough to fit four football fields. It had 48 checkout lanes and 2,000 shopping carts. The new store expected to see approximately 60,000 shoppers each week. The article reported shoppers seemed happy with the store. One shopper raved, "The low prices alone would make it worthwhile, but the variety is great."[5]

CHAPTER
EIGHT

LATER YEARS

By the 1980s, Walmarts were becoming common around the country. But Walton was just stepping onto the public scene. In October 1985, *Forbes* magazine named Walton the richest man in America. This sparked a string of interest from the media in Walton and his family.

Many people were surprised by Walton's frugal and simple lifestyle despite the amount of money he had. Walton and Helen quickly became annoyed by the media attention. It bothered Walton that people seemed to be prying into his family's finances. He noted the reporters who wanted to do stories on him never actually seemed to care about Walmart, the thing that had made him his money. And Walton did not enjoy talking about himself.

It also irritated Walton that people he'd never met would write him letters asking for money. He once said, "I remember one letter from a woman who just came right out and said, 'I've never been able to afford

Walton enjoyed taking an active role in the Walmart corporation until health issues forced him to slow down.

> "[People] make a big deal about Sam being a billionaire and driving an old pickup truck or buying his clothes at Walmart or refusing to fly first class. It's just the way we were brought up. When a penny is lying out there on the street, how many people would go out there and pick it up? I'll bet I would. And I know Sam would."[3]
>
> —Bud Walton

the $100,000 house I've always wanted. Will you give me the money?'"[1]

Charity

Although Walton and his family did not believe in giving handouts to random people, they did believe in donating to worthy causes. Helen especially pushed her husband to donate to more causes. Walton was principally interested in charities that promoted education. He confided in his autobiography that he believed education is the key to being competitive in a global market. He believed in people making something of themselves through hard work and dedication. As he grew older, Walton became especially concerned about the state of education in inner city and rural schools.

In 1981, Walmart created the Walmart Foundation. The foundation would manage the company's charitable donations and activities. The first year, the foundation gave $65,000 to charity. This was approximately 0.1 percent of the company's income that year.[2]

But contributions from the Walmart Foundation increased as time went on. In 2011, the foundation gave $958.9 million in contributions to various causes around the world, including education, hunger relief, environmental causes, and workforce development.[4] Since its beginnings, the foundation has encouraged Walmart employees to get involved in charity activities. While the Walmart Foundation is mainly funded through the company, Walton also started the Walton

GIVING TOO LITTLE?

Walmart was sometimes criticized for not giving enough money to charity. For example, in 1987, Walmart donated $4.3 million, 0.4 percent of the company's annual earnings. That same year, Kmart, Walmart's main competitor, gave 1.5 percent of its sales to charity. Also in 1987, Sears gave 2.4 percent. Dayton-Hudson, which owned Target and several other types of stores, gave 3.8 percent to charity.[5] Walmart also had a habit of loudly publicizing its donations. And, since many Walmarts were located in small towns, the donations seemed very large when compared with donations of the small local stores.

To some, this made Walmart look cheap and selfish. But Walton did not like the company to give away much money. He tried to explain his reasoning in his autobiography:

We feel very strongly that Walmart really is not, and should not be, in the charity business. We don't believe in taking a lot of money out of Walmart's cash registers and giving it to charity for the simple reason that any debit has to be passed along to somebody—either our shareholders or our customers.[6]

At times, Walmart has endured criticism for hourly wages paid to employees.

Family Foundation, another charity organization, which is funded through the Walton family's money.

Walmart Supercenter

In 1988, Walton oversaw what would be the last big Walmart project of his life—the Walmart Supercenter. The idea came from earlier experiments with the Hypermarts. The first Walmart Supercenter opened in Washington, Missouri, in March 1988. It was 120,000 square feet (36,576 sq m) and had 24 registers.[7] It was Walton's idea to have many checkout lanes. If people had to wait in line for a long time their frozen goods might thaw, he noted. This prototype store sold groceries as well as the household items available at regular Walmart stores. The store also had a pharmacy, an optical store, a garden center, and snack bars. Walton predicted Walmart Supercenters would be very popular in the future. Supercenters would become the main focus of Walmart's growth as it continued expanding.

Facing Bad News

One day in November 1989, Walton returned from quail hunting to his hunting trailer only to find that he had locked himself out. With the assistance of his dog handler, Walton was able to get into the trailer through a small upper window. But as he tried to squeeze through, his dog whistle hanging around his neck got stuck on the window. The whistle was pressed against his sternum. He was surprised by how much it hurt. And his ribs felt very sore the next day. His arm began to ache as well.

Walton decided to see his doctor in Houston, who had been treating him for hairy cell leukemia. It was discovered Walton had cancer in his bone marrow called multiple myeloma. This time, Walton did not waste any time getting treatment. He started chemotherapy and radiation treatment immediately. But the cancer was advanced and very difficult to treat successfully.

In January 16, 1990, Walton sent out a letter to all Walmart employees explaining the situation. In the letter, he was hopeful about his recovery and looking forward to visiting more Walmart stores within a month or so. And sure enough, whenever his doctors would allow him, Walton went about his Walmart business. On January 26, he visited a Walmart and told a reporter, "I've been on this treatment for about a week now and there seems to be a

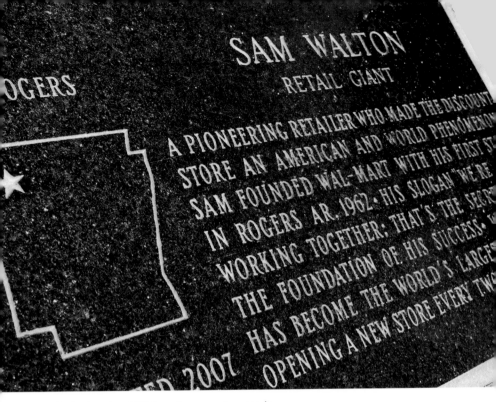

At the height of Walmart's expansion, Walton was opening a new store every two business days.

definite improvement in the way I feel and the way I'm walking."[9]

But in private, Walton was often in extreme pain. The chemotherapy and radiation helped, but only temporarily. He began going into work at 7 a.m. instead of his usual 5 a.m. Then, he would leave the office at noon to rest. It soon became clear Walton was not going to get better. He finally had to stop visiting stores at the end of 1991. But, with his mind still sharp, he would not be content to sit around and do nothing.

CHAPTER
NINE

LEAVING A LEGACY

With his health failing as he suffered from cancer, Walton felt compelled to write his autobiography. He had already started working on one a few years earlier, but since he did not like to talk about his personal life much, he had shrugged it off. Plus, he had wanted to focus on visiting Walmart stores while he still could.

Now, he threw himself into the project and found a coauthor in John Huey, a writer for *Fortune* magazine. It was important to Walton that people get the real story of his life and Walmart as he saw it. Although his body was suffering, the book project gave him something to focus on and lifted his spirits. He wrote in the autobiography's introduction:

> So I'm going to try to tell this story the best I'm able to, as close to the way it all came about, and I hope it will be almost as interesting and fun and exciting as it's been for all of us, and that I can capture for you at least something of the spirit we've all felt in building this company. More than anything, though, I want to get

Mere days before Walton's death, President George H. W. Bush presented him with the Presidential Medal of Freedom for his vast achievements in business.

85

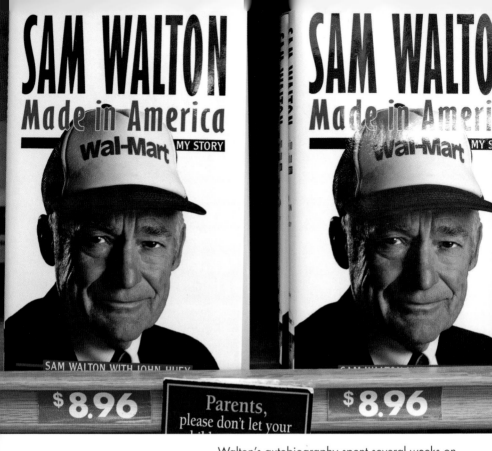

SAM WALTON
Made in America
Wal-Mart MY STORY

SAM WALTON WITH JOHN HUEY

$8.96

Parents,
please don't let your

SAM WALTON
Made in Ameri
Wal-Mart MY S

$8.96

Walton's autobiography spent several weeks on
the *New York Times* Best-Seller List.

across once and for all just how important Walmart's
associates have been to its success.[1]

Walton's autobiography is titled *Sam Walton: Made in*
America, and it was published in 1991. The book became
a national bestseller. Walton noted within the book
that at least some of the proceeds generated from book
sales would be donated to charities, including the New
American School Corporation, which was raising money
for public school reform.

A Fond Farewell

On March 17, 1992, Walton received his greatest honor yet. President George H. W. Bush presented him with the Presidential Medal of Freedom. The award ceremony took place in Bentonville in the Walmart offices' auditorium. Walton invited hundreds of associates to witness the event. He had to be brought onstage in a wheelchair, but he stood to receive his award and wave to the crowd. In return, the crowd gave Walton a standing ovation.

Only days later, Walton was hospitalized at the University of Arkansas hospital in Little Rock. Unfortunately, it was there he finally lost his battle to cancer. Walton died on the morning of April 5. He was 74 years old.

Walmart Today

Today, Walmart has grown beyond what Walton and many

HOPE FOR HIS DESCENDANTS

Because Walton worked hard for his living, he worried his descendants might just live off the money they would inherit from the Walton family. He explained, "I do admit to worrying sometimes about future generations of the Waltons. I know it's unrealistic of me to expect them all to get up and throw paper routes, and I know it's something I can't control. But I'd hate to see any descendants of mine fall into the category of what I'd call 'idle rich'—a group I've never had much use for."[2]

others ever imagined. In the United States alone, Walmart had five different types of stores in 2012. Many of them remain similar to the models originally envisioned by Walton.

Walmart Supercenters sell general products, including apparel, toys, and home goods as well as groceries. Most Supercenters also have pharmacies, banks, and fast-food restaurants inside. Some of them have hair and nail salons and vision centers or health clinics. Supercenters are big, usually more than 180,000 square feet (54,864 sq m). Many are open 24 hours a day. As of 2012, there were more than 3,000 Supercenters in the United States and many more throughout the world.[3]

Walmart's claim to fame is its background in discounting, and discounting is still important to the

Walmart stores, such as this one in China, offer discounted merchandise to shoppers in nearly 70 different countries.

Walmart vision. Walmart Discount Stores are similar to the original Walmart stores that became popular before Supercenters expanded. They are smaller than Supercenters and do not sell groceries. As of 2012, there were more than 600 of these stores in the United States.[5]

Walmart Neighborhood Markets are Supercenters on a much smaller scale. The first Neighborhood Market opened in 1998. These stores offer fresh groceries as well as household items and a pharmacy. In 2012, Walmart operated approximately 200 of these stores in the United States.

The first Walmart Express opened in 2011. These stores are usually placed in urban and rural areas that are far from larger Walmart stores. At only 15,000 square feet (4,572 sq m), these stores offer general merchandise, food items, and a pharmacy.

Sam's Club has stayed true to Walton's original vision and has been quite successful. In fiscal year 2012, Sam's Club made a total of $53 billion in sales. Many Sam's Clubs have pharmacies, photo centers, vision centers, and tire and battery centers for cars. As of 2012, there were more than 600 Sam's Clubs in the United States and approximately 100 Sam's Clubs outside the country.[6]

Growing Criticisms

As Walmart grew more and more successful, some people began questioning some of the company's business tactics and its effect on small communities. The bulk of these criticisms occurred after Walton's death. One main concern was the impact Walmarts had on the small towns they were often built in. Local merchants could not compete with Walmart's low prices and sometimes had to close as the result of a Walmart coming into town. Kenneth Stone, an economics professor at Iowa State University, dedicated years to studying this problem. He noted in one essay, "There is strong evidence that rural communities in the United States have been more adversely impacted by the discount of mass merchandisers—sometimes referred to as the Walmart phenomenon—than by any other factor."[8] Although Walton insisted in his autobiography that Walmarts would not be built in communities that did not want them, there is little evidence that communities were often able to prevent Walmarts from being built in their towns.

Another concern is where the goods sold at Walmart are made. The vast majority of products are made in

China where labor costs are generally cheaper than in the United States. In 2002, Walmart opened its own office in Shenzhen, China, where merchandisers try to get their products into Walmart stores in the United States. Within two years, approximately 80 percent of Walmart's foreign merchandisers were located in China.[9] Some people object to this practice because they believe it takes jobs away from people in

OUTSOURCING TO CHINA

In the last few decades, China has become the main supplier of products sold in the United States. Many products that were originally invented and made in the United States are now manufactured in China, including Levi's jeans, Radio Flyer wagons, Etch-A-Sketch toys, and even some American flag pins.

The main reason companies decide to have goods made in China is because it is often cheaper. For example, a Chicago company that creates fans, space heaters, and humidifiers, called Lakewood Engineering and Manufacturing Co., discovered in 2000 when facing large orders of goods that they could get more products assembled for cheaper in China than the United States. While Lakewood had to pay approximately $13 per hour to US employees, workers in China were paid only approximately 25¢ per hour of work.[10] By offering the lowest prices around, Walmart often supports importing goods from China.

Some argue that importing goods from China hurts the US economy. Others worry about the quality of life for Chinese workers. As *Businessweek* reported in 1999, at one Chinese factory that supplies goods for Walmart, employees worked in a windowless factory all day with only 60 minutes to leave for lunch. Workers could be punched or hit for misbehavior and fined for taking a long bathroom break.

the United States. But most economists believe this is actually healthy international trade that strengthens the US economy. And, the money saved from buying products cheaply is often passed down to the customer. Being able to buy products for less is especially helpful for low-income Americans.

Additionally, some people have concerns about the treatment of Chinese workers who produce goods for Walmart. They believe Walmart is exploiting these workers by paying them low wages and treating them badly. But some experts point to the fact that factory jobs in China are much better than some other jobs there. Shutting down factories could actually hurt people because they might be forced to

WALMARTS AROUND THE WORLD

Walmart has become a global company. As of 2012, Walmart had stores in 27 different countries under 69 different names and types.[11] Some of the stores are big discount stores similar to the Walmart Walton developed. But others are restaurants, smaller supermarkets, or Hypermarts. For example, in Guatemala Walmart owns four types of stores: Despensa Familia, a smaller store that sells food items; Paiz, a larger store that sells food and general merchandise; Walmart Supercenter, similar to the US model, a giant store that sells groceries and merchandise; and ClubCo, which is similar to Sam's Club in the United States. Although only one of the stores is named Walmart, they are all owned by the same company.

take on even tougher work or be unable to find work at all.

Moving Forward

Despite the criticism, it is true Sam Walton changed the way mass retail operates in the United States. He gave small towns more choice of products by building Walmarts, which also brought in business from neighboring towns. He worked hard to always offer customers the lowest price on everything his stores sold. And, by playing by his own set of rules, he changed the way people think about retail.

Starting with one small store in one small town, Walton became the founder of the largest retailer in the world. Walton's work ethic and strong desire to connect with customers and motivate employees will not soon be forgotten.

Walton speaks to an assembly of Walmart associates
while accepting a medal from the president.

TIMELINE

1918
Sam Walton is born on March 29.

1936
Walton begins college at the University of Missouri.

1940
Walton graduates from college with a degree in business in June.

1940
On June 3, Walton starts working for J. C. Penney in Des Moines, Iowa.

1942
Walton joins the army but is relegated to a noncombat position.

1943
On Valentine's Day, Walton marries Helen Robson. World War II ends. Walton is discharged from his military duties.

1945

Walton purchases his first Ben Franklin franchise in Newport, Arkansas.

1950

Walton and his family move to Bentonville, Arkansas, and open Walton's Five and Dime.

1962

On July 2, Walton opens the first Walmart in Rogers, Arkansas.

1968

Walton hires Ron Mayer to bring more computer technology to Walmart's processes.

1970

On October 1, Walmart becomes a public company.

1974

In November, Walton resigns from his position as CEO. Mayer becomes CEO.

TIMELINE

1976
Walton takes back his old job as Walmart's CEO in June.

1979
Walmart hits $1 billion in sales.

1982
Walton is diagnosed with hairy cell leukemia.

1983
The first Sam's Club opens.

1984
Walton has Glass and Shewmaker switch jobs. Many believe Walton is grooming Glass to take over as CEO.

1985
Forbes magazine names Walton the richest man in America.

1987

The first Hypermart USA opens in December near Dallas, Texas.

1988

In March, the first Walmart Supercenter opens in Washington, Missouri.

1989

Walton discovers he has multiple myeloma.

1992

On March 17, Walton receives the Presidential Medal of Freedom.

1992

Walton dies on April 5.

ESSENTIAL FACTS

Date of Birth
March 29, 1918

Place of Birth
near Kingfisher, Oklahoma

Date of Death
April 5, 1992

Parents
Tom Walton and Nancy "Nan" Walton

Education
University of Missouri

Marriage
Helen Robson (February 14, 1943)

Children
Samuel ("Rob") Robson, John Thomas, James Carr,
Alice Louise

Career Highlights

Starting with a single Ben Franklin store franchise in Newport, Arkansas, in 1945, Walton used his business savvy and strong leadership to grow a retail empire that changed the way people shop. Walmart surpassed $1 billion in annual sales by 1979. Walton was awarded the Presidential Medal of Freedom on March 17, 1992.

Societal Contribution

Walton and Walmart have contributed to various organizations around the world. Walmart is supportive of its associates volunteering for charity organizations.

Conflicts

Walton faced several health conflicts throughout his life, suffering from both hairy cell leukemia and bone cancer. Walton and his family also struggled with the fame and attention that came from founding Walmart.

Quote

"Each Walmart store should reflect the values of its customers and support the vision they hold for their community."—*Sam Walton*

GLOSSARY

buyer
The person in charge of purchasing merchandise to sell in a store.

camaraderie
Trust and friendship between two people or a group of people.

drove
A large group of people.

enterprise
A business undertaking.

fiscal year
A period of 12 months, which may differ from a standard year on the calendar, during which a company is able to use funds.

franchise
The license given to a person or group to use a company's name or sell its goods in a specified region.

lease
An agreement between a landlord and a renter that includes information about how long a property can be occupied by the renter and other conditions related to renting.

notorious
Widely known.

repossess
To reclaim something.

rigorous
Challenging or hard work.

skeptical
Unsure or questioning.

surplus
An extra amount of something.

valedictorian
The student with the highest grades in a graduating class.

vie
To work toward victory or superiority.

wholesale
Selling in large quantities.

ADDITIONAL RESOURCES

Selected Bibliography

Bianco, Anthony. *Walmart: The Bully of Bentonville*. New York: Doubleday, 2006. Print.

Ortega, Bob. *In Sam We Trust: The Untold Story of Sam Walton and Walmart, the World's Most Powerful Retailer*. New York: Three Rivers, 2000. Print.

Walton, Sam, and John Huey. *Sam Walton: Made in America*. New York: Bantam, 1992. Print.

Further Readings

Bergdahl, Michael. *The Sam Walton Way: "50 of Mr. Sam's Best Leadership Practices."* Chandler, AZ: Brighton, 2011. Print.

Blumenthal, Karen. *Mr. Sam: How Sam Walton Built Walmart and Became America's Richest Man*. New York: Viking Juvenile, 2011. Print.

Web Sites

To learn more about Sam Walton, visit ABDO Publishing Company online at **www.abdopublishing.com**. Web sites about Sam Walton are featured on our Book Links page. These links are routinely monitored and updated to provide the most current information available.

Places to Visit

University of Missouri
Office of Visitor Relations
104 Jesse Hall
Columbia, MO 65211
573-882-6333
http://www.missouri.edu/visitors/index.php?lid=aud
Sam Walton attended the University of Missouri and
majored in economics. Visitors can tour the school where
Walton spent many years and prepared for his career.

Walmart Visitor Center
105 N. Main Street
Bentonville, AR 72712
479-273-1329
http://corporate.walmart.com/our-story/heritage
/visitor center
The visitor center is located in the first Walton's Five &
Dime. Visitors can see the original storefront and how
the store was set up when it first opened. There is also an
interactive gallery where visitors can learn about Walmart's
history.

SOURCE NOTES

Chapter 1. A New Opportunity

1. Sam Walton and John Huey. *Sam Walton: Made in America*. New York: Bantam, 1992. Print. 22.

2. Ibid. 24.

3. Ibid. 27.

4. Bob Ortega. *In Sam We Trust: The Untold Story of Sam Walton and Wal-Mart, the World's Most Powerful Retailer*. New York: Three Rivers, 2000. Print. 27.

5. Sam Walton and John Huey. *Sam Walton: Made in America*. New York: Bantam, 1992. Print. 28.

6. Ibid. 30.

Chapter 2. Southern Upbringing

1. Vance H. Trimble. *Sam Walton: The Inside Story of America's Richest Man*. New York: Penguin, 1990. Print. 22.

2. Sam Walton and John Huey. *Sam Walton: Made in America*. New York: Bantam, 1992. Print. 5.

3. Ibid. 12.

4. Vance H. Trimble. *Sam Walton: The Inside Story of America's Richest Man*. New York: Penguin, 1990. Print. 26.

5. Sam Walton and John Huey. *Sam Walton: Made in America*. New York: Bantam, 1992. Print. 15.

6. Ibid. 16.

7. Ibid.

8. Ibid. 15.

Chapter 3. J. C. Penney and World War II

1. Bob Ortega. *In Sam We Trust: The Untold Story of Sam Walton and Wal-Mart, the World's Most Powerful Retailer*. New York: Three Rivers, 2000. Print. 22.

2. Sam Walton and John Huey. *Sam Walton: Made In America*. New York: Bantam, 1992. Print. 17.

3. Vance H. Trimble. *Sam Walton: The Inside Story of America's Richest Man*. New York: Penguin, 1990. Print. 34.

4. Ibid.

Chapter 4. A Second Try

1. Sam Walton and John Huey. *Sam Walton: Made In America*. New York: Bantam, 1992. Print. 32.

2. Ibid. 39.

3. Ibid. 44.

4. Ibid. 43.

5. Bob Ortega. *In Sam We Trust: The Untold Story of Sam Walton and Wal-Mart, the World's Most Powerful Retailer*. New York: Three Rivers, 2000. Print. 56.

6. Ibid. 55.

Chapter 5. Walmart Expands

1. Sam Walton and John Huey. *Sam Walton: Made in America*. New York: Bantam, 1992. Print. 50.

2. Bob Ortega. *In Sam We Trust: The Untold Story of Sam Walton and Wal-Mart, the World's Most Powerful Retailer*. New York: Three Rivers, 2000. Print. 57.

3. Sam Walton and John Huey. *Sam Walton: Made in America*. New York: Bantam, 1992. Print. 45–46.

4. Ibid. 89.

5. Ibid. 49.

6. Ibid. 55.

7. Bob Ortega. *In Sam We Trust: The Untold Story of Sam Walton and Wal-Mart, the World's Most Powerful Retailer*. New York: Three Rivers, 2000. Print. 56.

8. Sam Walton and John Huey. *Sam Walton: Made in America*. New York: Bantam, 1992. Print. 66.

9. Ibid. 60.

10. Bob Ortega. *In Sam We Trust: The Untold Story of Sam Walton and Wal-Mart, the World's Most Powerful Retailer*. New York: Three Rivers, 2000. Print. 62.

11. Sam Walton and John Huey. *Sam Walton: Made in America*. New York: Bantam, 1992. Print. 69.

SOURCE NOTES CONTINUED

Chapter 6. Growth Strategy

1. Sam Walton and John Huey. *Sam Walton: Made in America.* New York: Bantam, 1992. Print. 99.

2. Ibid.

3. Vance H. Trimble. *Sam Walton: The Inside Story of America's Richest Man.* New York: Penguin, 1990. Print. 119.

4. Bob Ortega. *In Sam We Trust: The Untold Story of Sam Walton and Wal-Mart, the World's Most Powerful Retailer.* New York: Three Rivers, 2000. Print. 78.

5. Ibid.

6. Sam Walton and John Huey. *Sam Walton: Made in America.* New York: Bantam, 1992. Print. 148.

7. Ibid. 151.

8. Ibid. 157.

9. Ibid. 152.

10. Ibid. 154.

11. Ibid. 196.

Chapter 7. New Enterprises, New Challenges

1. Vance H. Trimble. *Sam Walton: The Inside Story of America's Richest Man.* New York: Penguin, 1990. Print. 203.

2. Ibid. 209.

3. Sam Walton and John Huey. *Sam Walton: Made in America.* New York: Bantam, 1992. Print. 187.

4. Vance H. Trimble. *Sam Walton: The Inside Story of America's Richest Man.* New York: Penguin, 1990. Print. 209.

5. Thomas C. Hayes. "The Hypermarket: 5 Acres of Store." *New York Times.* New York Times, 4 Feb. 1988. Web. 3 Feb. 2013.

Chapter 8. Later Years

1. Sam Walton and John Huey. *Sam Walton: Made in America.* New York: Bantam, 1992. Print. 2.

2. Bob Ortega. *In Sam We Trust: The Untold Story of Sam Walton and Wal-Mart, the World's Most Powerful Retailer.* New York: Three Rivers, 2000. Print. 195.

3. Sam Walton and John Huey. *Sam Walton: Made in America.* New York: Bantam, 1992. Print. 5.

4. "Community Giving." *Walmart.* Walmart, 10 Dec. 2012. Web. 3 Feb. 2013.

5. Bob Ortega. *In Sam We Trust: The Untold Story of Sam Walton and Wal-Mart, the World's Most Powerful Retailer.* New York: Three Rivers, 2000. Print. 195.

6. Sam Walton and John Huey. *Sam Walton: Made in America.* New York: Bantam, 1992. Print. 240.

7. Vance H. Trimble. *Sam Walton: The Inside Story of America's Richest Man.* New York: Penguin, 1990. Print. 296.

8. Ibid. 301.

9. Ibid. 302.

Chapter 9. Leaving a Legacy

1. Sam Walton and John Huey. *Sam Walton: Made in America.* New York: Bantam, 1992. Print. xii.

2. Ibid. 76.

3. "Walmart U.S. Stores." *Walmart.* Walmart, 2012. Web. 15 Dec. 2012.

4. Sam Walton and John Huey. *Sam Walton: Made in America.* New York: Bantam, 1992. Print. 331.

5. "Walmart U.S. Stores." *Walmart.* Walmart, 2012. Web. 15 Dec. 2012.

6. Ibid.

7. "Our Stores." *Walmart.* Walmart, n.d. Web. 14 Dec. 2012.

8. Anthony Bianco. *Wal-Mart: The Bully of Bentonville.* New York: Doubleday, 2006. Print. 141–142.

9. Ibid. 187.

10. Ibid. 186.

11. "Our Stores." *Walmart.* Walmart, n.d. Web. 14 Dec. 2012.

INDEX

ABOUT THE AUTHOR

Katherine Krieg is the author and editor of many fiction and nonfiction books for young people. Krieg is pursuing a Master of Fine Arts degree in creative writing.

ABOUT THE CONSULTANT

Art Carden is an assistant professor of economics at Samford University in Birmingham, Alabama, a senior research fellow with the Institute for Faith, Work, and Economics, a research fellow with the Independent Institute, a senior fellow with the Beacon Center of Tennessee, and a regular contributor to Forbes.com and the *Washington Examiner*. His research interests include the economic history of the American South, economic development more generally, and all things related to Walmart.